P9-CPY-332

COMMUNITIES

Urban Canada

DENNIS DESRIVIERES

SUSAN ALIPHAT

COLIN BAIN

GRAHAM JARVIS

ANGUS SCULLY

CONTENTS

Prentice Hall Ginn Canada
Scarborough, Ontario

THE GROWTH OF COMMUNITIES

About a century ago, most people in Canada lived on farms or in forests, and spent much of their working day out-of-doors. Today, three out of four Canadians live in communities, the majority of them in cities. Almost half of Canada's population is clustered in the nation's ten largest metropolitan centres alone! For most Canadians, outdoor experience is limited to summer camping and winter sports. We live and work in **urban** places.

In Canada, an urban place is a community with 1000 or more people and a density of at least 400 people per square kilometre. Urban places include four types of communities: villages, towns, cities, and metropolitan areas. **Metropolitan areas** — cities and nearby areas with a total of 100 000 people or more — are growing fastest. Between 1951 and 1991, the ten largest metropolitan areas increased in population by over 250 percent.

Rapid urban growth — **urbanization** — has brought many changes with it. In this booklet, you will examine why cities have grown and how they operate. You will also plan ways to improve communities for the people in them. Begin by answering these questions, using the information on these two pages.

- What is meant by the terms **urbanization** and **urban places**?

- What proportion of Canadians live in urban places? Suggest three reasons why the number is high.

- Describe the location of Canada's major centres. How does their location relate to the Canada/United States border?

- Which large urban places grew fastest between 1951 and 1991? Which grew more slowly?

- Which of the ten metropolitan centres is closest to your home? How does it influence your community?

Key Words

- ◆ urban
- ◆ urbanization
- ◆ site
- ◆ geographic inertia
- ◆ service orders
- ◆ new towns
- ◆ radial street pattern
- ◆ grid street pattern
- ◆ land-use maps

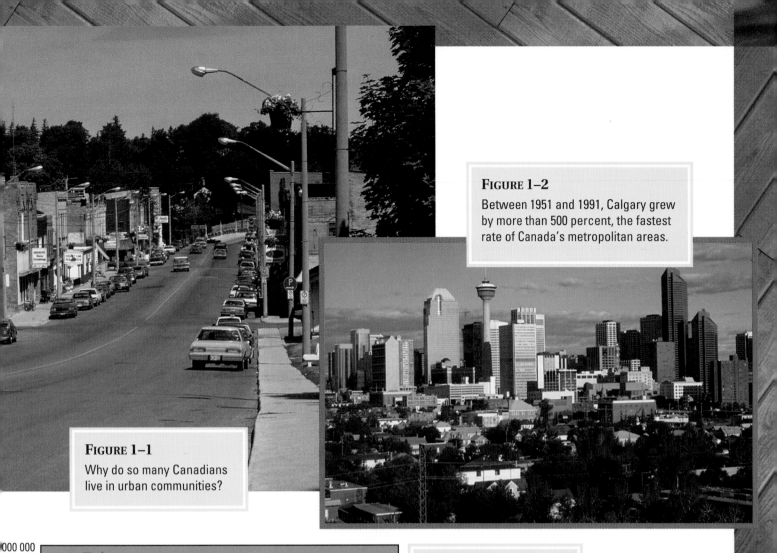

FIGURE 1–2

Between 1951 and 1991, Calgary grew by more than 500 percent, the fastest rate of Canada's metropolitan areas.

FIGURE 1–1

Why do so many Canadians live in urban communities?

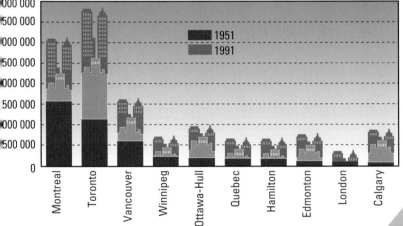

FIGURE 1–3

Population of metropolitan areas in Canada

Legend: 1951, 1991

X-axis: Montreal, Toronto, Vancouver, Winnipeg, Ottawa-Hull, Quebec, Hamilton, Edmonton, London, Calgary

Y-axis: 0, 500 000, 1 000 000, 1 500 000, 2 000 000, 2 500 000, 3 000 000, 3 500 000, 4 000 000

Looking Forward

- Why are communities located at certain types of sites?

- How do communities grow, and what factors help them to survive?

- What sorts of services are provided by cities, towns, and villages, and how large are the areas they serve?

- What different types of street plans are evident in Canadian communities?

- How should land uses be arranged in a model community?

FIGURE 1–4

Canada's largest metropolitan areas. Why do you think metropolitan centres have grown rapidly?

Communities Always Change

Communities are constantly changing. Farms are sold, and new homes take their place. Resource industries prosper, then they're gone. People move away, new families from other places come in. New highways are built, but the railway tracks are pulled up. Businesses come, businesses go. Some communities grow into large cities, while others quietly fade to ghost towns.

FIGURE 1–5
The different architectural styles we see in our communities reflect changes that have gone on through the decades.

Communities in the Past

People have lived together in urban places for 10 000 years or more. Communities formed when cultures stored or traded surplus food to support inhabitants through the winter months. Surplus food also fed townspeople who had little time to produce their own food, people such as skilled artisans, healers, soldiers, and leaders. The largest Aboriginal villages and towns in prehistoric Canada were based on salmon on the West Coast, and on corn crops in the Great Lakes-St. Lawrence region. These early communities belonged to widespread trade networks. Complex village societies were built upon a steady supply of food.

Later, European settlers built communities at safe harbours along the Atlantic coast and along river valleys, such as the St. John and the St. Lawrence, that led into Canada. Some settlements, such as Montreal, grew in stages to become major cities. Others either remained small or no longer exist.

FIGURE 1–6
Artist's impression of Kitkatla, a Tsimshian village in British Columbia before contact with Europeans. What evidence can you see of skilled craftspeople in this community?

FIGURE 1–7

Source: Adapted from The Toronto Star, March 3, 1991.

The Old House: Most communities still have buildings from earlier days that can tell a great deal about the community's past. Unscramble the story of the Old House in these pictures, and identify ways in which the area changed as a large city grew.

Approximations of Community Sizes in Canada*	
Hamlet	Clusters of fewer than 200 people
Village	From 200 to 1000people
Town	From 1000 to 10 000 people
Small city	From 10 000 to 50 000 people
City	More than 50 000 people
Metropolitan Area	A city and nearby area, with at least 100 000 people

*Village, town, and city status are set by legal acts of incorporation rather than by population levels. Metropolitan areas are identified by the Census of Canada.

Site Is Important

Site is the term used to describe the specific spot where an urban place is located. For example, communities such as Kitkatla village in Figure 1–6 were established near a protected natural harbour along a shoreline or river. Six other types of sites are shown in Figure 1–8.

Many of Canada's large cities have different types of sites. For example, Victoria, British Columbia, and St. John's, Newfoundland, grew around sheltered natural harbours. Quebec City is both a defensive and a corridor site; guns on its high cliffs once controlled entry to the St. Lawrence Valley. Winnipeg, Manitoba, grew where a fur-trade post was located at the junction of the Red and Assiniboine rivers. Niagara Falls, Ontario, is an excellent example of a city located at a power site.

FIGURE 1–8

Six types of community sites. Match the visual examples to the types of sites.

Sites determined by transportation factors

Junction site: A point where two or more transport lines meet.

Crossing site: A point where a water body or river is easiest to cross.

Gap/Corridor site: A point at the entrance or exit of a valley, canyon, or mountain pass.

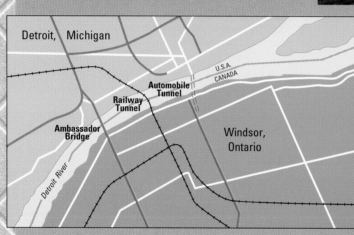

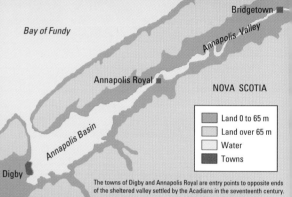

Sites determined by other factors

Defensive site: A point that gives some strategic control over an area, such as a commanding view.

Power-source site: A point where water power is available for industrial use.

Resource-based site: A point at which it is easy to gather a natural resource.

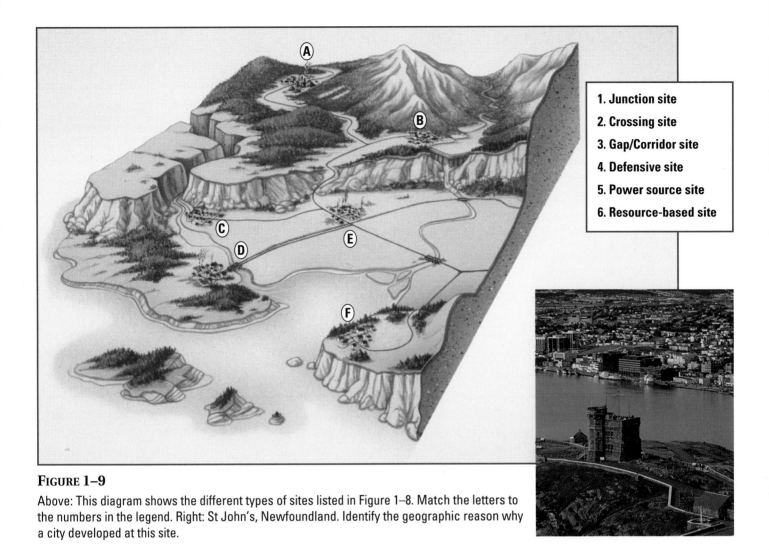

1. Junction site
2. Crossing site
3. Gap/Corridor site
4. Defensive site
5. Power source site
6. Resource-based site

FIGURE 1–9

Above: This diagram shows the different types of sites listed in Figure 1–8. Match the letters to the numbers in the legend. Right: St John's, Newfoundland. Identify the geographic reason why a city developed at this site.

Activities

1. a) In your notebook, list the correct order of pictures showing the Old House. How did the Old House change through the years?
    b) Identify these stages in the growth of the Old House community: hamlet, village, town, city, and metropolis. Make an organizer to show the type of businesses and services that can be seen in each stage.
    c) Compare the forms of power, transportation, and building materials used as this community developed.

2. Write an opinion letter about the demolition of the Old House to this community's newspaper editor. Follow one of these arguments: "Save the Old House because…" or "Tear down the Old House because…."

3. a) Define "site," and give an example from your region.
    b) Carefully examine the visuals in Figure 1–8 to match each one with one of the six types of site. Decide which of these site types are most important today. Which are less important now? Why?

c) Use atlas maps to identify site factors for Edmonton, Montreal, Sudbury, Toronto, and Halifax.

4. Make a large copy of Figure 1–9 on blank paper.
    a) Identify the type of community site shown at each of the lettered locations.
    b) Locate the site on the diagram that you think would be the best place for a city to develop. Explain the advantages of your city site.
    c) Outline the boundaries of your community as it grows from village to town to city.
    d) Plan a road system to connect your city to other locations on the diagram that you think will become important towns. Name the places in the area.
    e) Complete your diagram with colour, legend, and title.

5. Take photographs or make sketches of different styles of homes and buildings in your community. Try to find out approximately when each of them was built. Prepare a display to show how the buildings in your community have changed over time.

Why Do Cities Grow?

Urban growth around the world has been one of the most striking geographical changes of the twentieth century. Why are cities growing? There are two main reasons: rural push and urban pull.

Rural push refers to conditions that force people to leave the land. Rural poverty and depleted natural resources such as the Atlantic cod fishery are examples. Labour-saving machinery that reduces the need for traditional work in farming and forestry is also a rural push.

Urban pull refers to factors that draw people to cities. A chance for a job attracts most people. The big centres often have employers in business, finance, government, and research. Other people seek opportunities to attend university or simply to be reunited with family and friends already in the city.

Immigration

FIGURE 1–10

Between 1880 and 1914, most immigrants to Canada came to farm on the Prairies. Suggest reasons why immigrants today are attracted to metropolitan centres.

Table 1–1 Fastest growing metropolitan areas of Canada, 1986–1991

City	5-year growth rate	Immigrant population, 1991*
Oshawa, Ontario	18%	17%
Vancouver, British Columbia	16	30
Kitchener, Ontario	14	22
Toronto, Ontario	13	38
Victoria, British Columbia	13	19
Ottawa-Hull, Ontario/Quebec	12	15
Calgary, Alberta	12	20
London, Ontario	11	18
Edmonton, Alberta	8	18
Halifax, Nova Scotia	8	6

* "Immigrants" defined as people born in a country outside Canada

Source: Jane Badets and Tina W.L. Chui, Canada's Changing Immigrant Population *(Statistics Canada/Prentice Hall Canada, 1994).*

Rural-to-Urban Shift

Table 1–2 Canadian population: Urban and rural, 1901–1991

Year	Urban	Rural farm	Rural non-farm
1901	52.7%	31.2%	16.1%
1911	54.5	27.1	18.4
1931	62.9	19.8	17.3
1951	69.6	11.4	19.0
1971	76.1	6.6	17.3
1981	75.7	4.3	20.0
1991	76.6	3.0	20.4

Source: Census of Canada.

FIGURE 1–11
Technology has raised farm output but reduced the need for agricultural workers. Only large farms can support the high costs of modern farming.

Changing Employment Patterns

FIGURE 1–12
Most of today's students will be employed in providing services rather than gathering resources or making products.

Table 1–3 Canadian workers by type of employment as a percentage of the labour force, 1901–2001 (estimated)

	Primary	Secondary	Tertiary/Quaternary
	(Primary harvesting: farms, fish, fur, forests, mines)	(Manufacturing and construction)	(Transportation, information, all services)
1901	44%	28%	28%
1921	36	27	37
1941	29	26	45
1961	17	32	51
1981	5	29	66
2001	4	20	76

Source: Ministry of Supply and Services, Canada Year Book, 1994.

Jobs in Urban Places

Many communities develop around a **primary industry** — that is, gathering resources such as grain, fish, or minerals. Others specialize in **secondary industry**, or manufacturing products. In any community, however, there are more people who work in providing services than in any other type of job. "Services" refers to all jobs where people do not harvest or mine resources or make products. Most services are also known as **tertiary industry**. **Quaternary services** are those, such as information technology, that require a high degree of specialized knowledge.

FIGURE 1–13
Identify primary, secondary, tertiary, and quaternary industry in these pictures. Give another example of each type.

Community Survey: Jobs

1. What is the approximate population of your community or the community nearest to your rural home?

2. Classify the community (see page 5):
   a) Hamlet
   b) Village
   c) Town
   d) City
   e) Metropolitan area

3. Have you ever had a part-time or summer job? If so, what type of job was it?

4. What are the main types of full-time jobs for which this area is known?

5. Do most people in the community work here? If not, where do they work?

6. For whom do people from this community work? Name the major employers.

7. Which of these types of services are found in the community? Give an example for each one that is present.
   a) Transportation
   b) Professional
   c) Financial
   d) Community services
   e) Government
   f) Personal services
   g) Public utilities
   h) Retailers

8. Are people in the community having difficulty finding jobs? Explain.

Providing Services

Communities are central places that provide services for the region around them. Villages offer only **low-order services** — services such as a post office or convenience store that people use often. Most people need to make only a short trip to use these services. Towns have both low- and **middle-order services**. A large grocery store will attract people into town for weekly shopping. Most towns have a secondary level school to which students are bussed from the surrounding rural area. Cities have three levels — low-, middle-, and **high-order services**. A high-quality department store will draw shoppers from a fairly wide area. Therefore, cities serve larger regions than towns, just as towns attract customers from larger areas than villages do. This principle helps explain the spacing of urban communities on a road map.

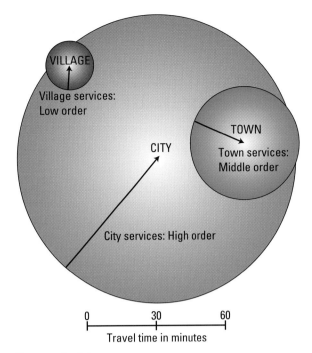

FIGURE 1–14

The distance people travel for different services

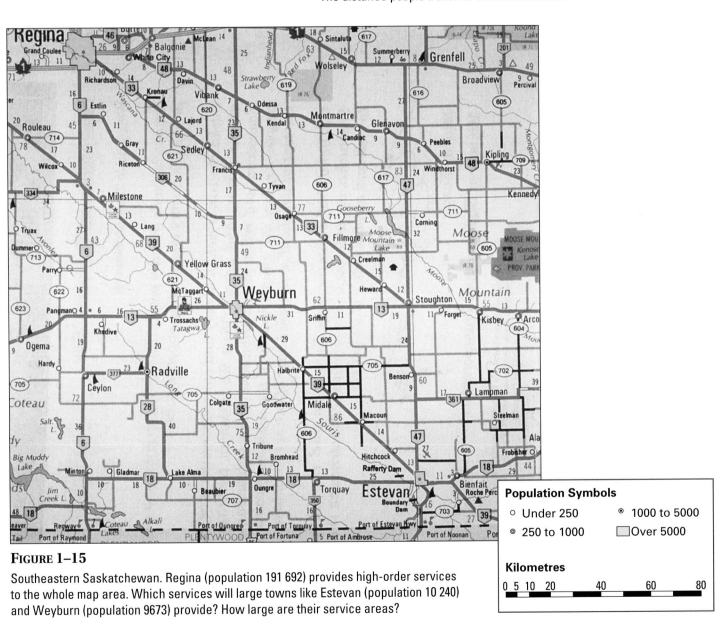

Population Symbols

- ○ Under 250
- ◉ 1000 to 5000
- ◉ 250 to 1000
- ▢ Over 5000

Kilometres

0 5 10 20   40   60   80

FIGURE 1–15

Southeastern Saskatchewan. Regina (population 191 692) provides high-order services to the whole map area. Which services will large towns like Estevan (population 10 240) and Weyburn (population 9673) provide? How large are their service areas?

Sarnia/Lambton:
A Community Built on Secondary Industry

The economy of the Sarnia/Lambton region of southwestern Ontario has been built on petroleum for more than a century. Canada's first oil wells were drilled at Oil Springs in 1859 and at nearby Petrolia a few years later. By 1880, Imperial Oil had established a refinery at Petrolia. It later relocated to the St. Clair River at Sarnia.

Today, only a trickle of Canada's oil comes from Ontario — less than one percent. Nevertheless, the petroleum and chemical industries in the Sarnia area continue, linked to Alberta by the Interprovincial Pipeline since 1953. More than three-quarters of Sarnia/Lambton's secondary industry is still based on petroleum and chemicals. Four major refineries process oil, while other industries make a wide range of chemical products from this resource.

Sarnia remains a petrochemical centre partly because of **geographic inertia**. This means that a business or industry remains in a community long after the original reasons for its location are gone. Recently, however, industry in "Chemical Valley" has been down-sized, and Sarnia/Lambton must now attract new jobs to survive.

FIGURE 1–16

Location of Sarnia/Lambton

FIGURE 1–17

Petrochemical industry in Sarnia/Lambton

"We've never been able to diversify. We've relied too heavily on one area. Everything should be in balance, so we don't suffer from ups and downs in the market. We've relied too much on the Chemical Valley. In the sixties and seventies, this area grew naturally on the petrochemical sector. At the time, people thought it would never end, but eventually, it did."

Mike Ireland, Sarnia/Lambton Economic Development Director

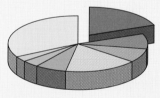

FIGURE 1–18

Sarnia/Lambton employment, 1991. Even in a community with specialized manufacturing, most people work at a wide variety of service jobs.

- Manufacturing (19.0%)
- Construction (9.0%)
- Primary resources (8.0%)
- All sales (17.0%)
- Other services (33.0%)
- Finances (3.0%)
- Government (4.0%)
- Transport/Utilities (7.0%)

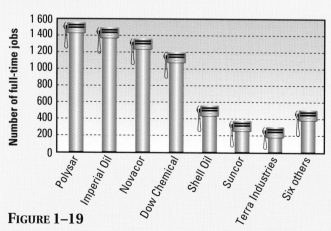

FIGURE 1–19

Petrochemical jobs and firms in Sarnia/Lambton, 1994

Table 1–4 Sarnia/Lambton manufacturing specialties. Where were most jobs lost between 1988 and 1994? How would job losses affect local merchants?

Manufacturing type	Number of employees 1988	1994
1. Petrochemicals	10 009	7 272
2. Metals, machinery	1 416	986
3. Wood products	235	185
4. Stone, clay, and glass	211	259
5. Textiles, leather goods	196	176
6. Food and beverages	21	172
7. Other manufactures	337	304
Total	12 425	9 374

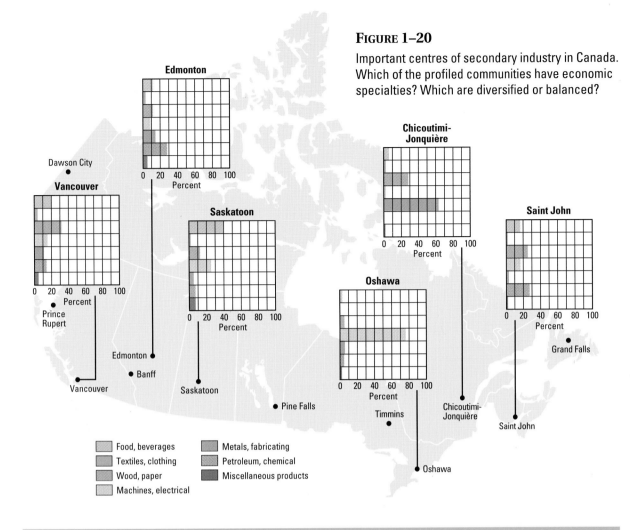

FIGURE 1–20

Important centres of secondary industry in Canada. Which of the profiled communities have economic specialties? Which are diversified or balanced?

Legend:
- Food, beverages
- Textiles, clothing
- Wood, paper
- Machines, electrical
- Metals, fabricating
- Petroleum, chemical
- Miscellaneous products

Activities

6. Work in a group of three. Look back at the section Why Do Cities Grow? (pages 8–9). Divide the three factors among group members.

   a) Students working on Table 1–1: Construct a multiple bar graph, using two colours or symbols for each city.

   b) Students working on Table 1–2 and Table 1–3: Construct a multiple line graph, using three colours or symbols to show the data.

   c) In your groups, describe the patterns in the graphs and suggest reasons for these patterns.

   d) Discuss how each graph adds to our under-standing of why and when urbanization has occurred in Canada.

7. a) Compare Sarnia/Lambton's employment data with data for your own community. List the similarities and differences.

   b) Describe how the loss of manufacturing jobs in a community affects:

      i)   the family   iv)   personal services
      ii) retail sales   v)   local government
      iii) real-estate prices

   c) Brainstorm a list of employment strategies for communities with problems resulting

from the loss of manufacturing jobs. Mike Ireland's comments are a good place to start.

8. a) Use the graphs in Figure 1–20 to identify the manufacturing specialties of the six cities featured. Which of these cities are similar to Sarnia? Which have more variety of employment?

   b) Examine atlas maps of natural resources and use the school library to find the employment base of the six other places shown on the map.

9. a) Use Figure 1–15 or a provincial road map of your own area to examine the spacing of communities. Start by making a simplified copy of the map area on blank paper. Omit all roads and the hamlets (the smallest places).

   b) Divide the low-order service areas among all villages, towns, and cities. Do this by finding the midpoint between adjacent places. Use one colour for these lines. Then use a second colour to divide middle-order service areas among the towns. Divide high-order services among any cities with a third colour.

   c) Describe and explain the pattern of your completed map.

Patterns Within Communities

Ouje'-Bougoumou is one of Canada's newest communities. It is a model of how people can plan and build new urban places, and it is the pride of Cree bands in central Quebec. Mining activity in the area forced these people to move several times during the past 60 years. Negotiations with the federal government finally established their Aboriginal claim to the area, and in 1990, planning of the village began. The circular plan focused on community services and was drawn up by the tribal elders.

Aboriginal architect Douglas Cardinal (designer of Canada's National Museum of Civilization in Ottawa-Hull) planned the central buildings based on traditional Cree forms. Residents built their own homes, all connected to one large furnace fuelled by sawdust waste from nearby mills. Ouje'-Bougoumou is a fresh start, planned and built by its residents.

This new Quebec village invites comparison with older communities in different regions of Canada. How are the streets, buildings, and parks arranged in urban places? How should the ideal community be organized?

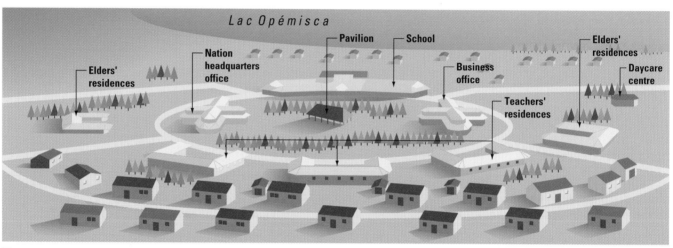

FIGURE 1–21

The village of Ouje'-Bougoumou. People began moving into homes in 1993.

Community Survey: Land Use and Street Patterns

1. Name the major intersection nearest to your home.

2. What is the name (if any) of your neighbourhood within the community?

3. Is your home:
   a) Low-density residential (detached house)
   b) Middle-density residential (duplex, townhouse)
   c) High-density residential (apartment)
   d) Rural agricultural (a farm)

4. How close do you live to the following areas of the community (or nearby community)?
   - **A block**
   - **A few blocks**
   - **A kilometre**
   - **More than a kilometre**

   a) Recreational: i) a local park
                    ii) a public arena
   b) Commercial: i) a convenience store
                    ii) "downtown" or a shopping centre
   c) Institutional: i) your school
                    ii) a public library

5. Describe the streets in your community.
   a) Streets mostly follow the shape of natural features such as hills, rivers, and lakes.
   b) Streets mostly are straight and form rectangular blocks.
   c) Streets mostly curve to form crescents and courts.
   d) The community has a mix of street patterns. (If so, which ones?)

Street Patterns Shape a Community

Radial Patterns

Street patterns can give a place a special character that makes urban living more pleasant. For example, Goderich, Ontario, calls itself "the prettiest town in Canada" because of its classic downtown street plan. The town was started by the Canada Company, a land company that brought British farmers to south-western Ontario. In 1827, they surveyed Goderich as their Lake Huron port and administrative centre. Goderich was given the **radial street pattern** of a European capital, although the site proved too isolated to become a city. Today, the plan draws traffic into the downtown area and helps promote the town as an attractive summer tourist centre.

FIGURE 1–22

Core area of Goderich, Ontario. Radiating streets focus on the county court house. In downtown Ottawa, major streets form a Y-pattern to highlight Canada's dramatic war memorial at Confederation Square. Does your community have any streets that converge on parks, public buildings, or monuments?

New Towns

There are many frontier resource communities far from the population centres of Canada. Many of them are **new towns**, places with a carefully planned system of streets and land uses aimed at improving community living. There are about 200 new towns in Canada, home to more than half a million people. Many of them were designed within the last 50 years by forest and mining companies.

Thompson, Manitoba, was planned as a mining and smelting town by the International Nickel Company (Inco) in 1957. Today, about 15 000 people live there. Curving **arterial streets** lead local traffic away from downtown into quiet neighbourhoods of crescents and courts (**cul-de-sacs**), often built around parks and schools. Many communities across Canada have neighbourhoods designed in the same way.

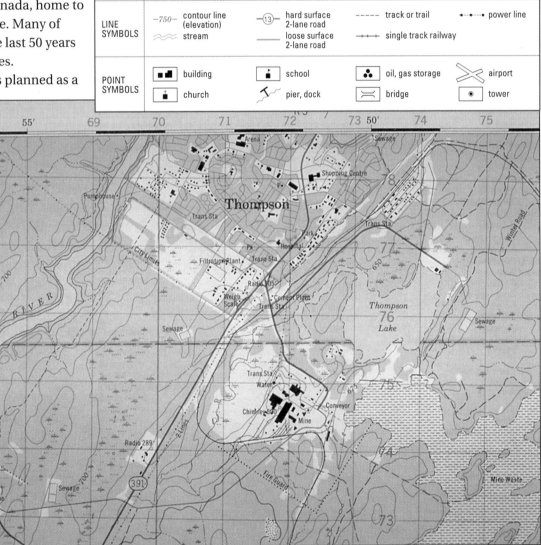

AREA SYMBOLS	water	wet, marsh	orchard	sand
	water-seasonally dry	forest	no trees	built-up area
LINE SYMBOLS	−750− contour line (elevation)	⑬ hard surface 2-lane road	----- track or trail	•-•-•-• power line
	stream	loose surface 2-lane road	+++++ single track railway	
POINT SYMBOLS	building	school	oil, gas storage	airport
	church	pier, dock	bridge	tower

FIGURE 1–23

Topographic map of Thompson, Manitoba. Scale: 1:55 000 (1 cm = .55 km). Note the street patterns. How does this pattern differ from the one in Goderich? Explain the advantages of planning residential streets in this way.

Grid Patterns

The **grid pattern** is the most common street system in Canadian communities. Here, straight streets cross one another at right angles. The Canadian Pacific Railway used this orderly street pattern in 1885 for Vancouver, the terminus of the first Canadian railway to reach the Pacific. At that time, the entire area was so heavily covered by huge Douglas firs that one surveyor became lost! It took three days to cut the first survey line from Burrard Inlet south across today's downtown core to the inlet at False Creek. Next, Granville Street was surveyed from this line as the main street. Finally, the rest of downtown Vancouver was laid out in a grid pattern based on Granville. This pattern of rectangles covers the Fraser River delta today (see page 44).

Most other railway towns and cities, such as Calgary, Lethbridge, Moose Jaw, Regina, Brandon, and Winnipeg, were planned the same way.

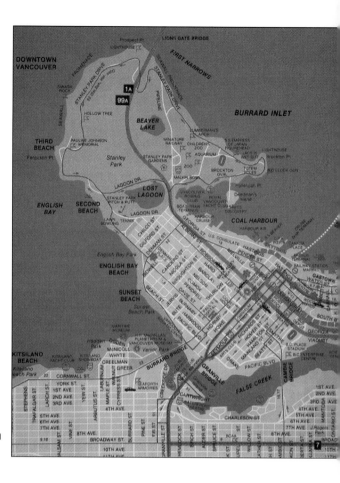

FIGURE 1-24

Downtown Vancouver. Describe the street pattern found in the downtown area of many communities.

Planning Better Communities

The Great Depression of the 1930s brought many social problems. Many Canadian communities were run-down and bankrupt. In 1935, architect and planner Humphrey Carver insisted that all Canadians had a right to live in safe, healthy, and comfortable homes. He argued that it was necessary to design better communities where people could lead good lives. Today, community planners prepare **land-use maps** to control and direct urban growth.

Land-use maps show the purpose of different areas of land. Residential, commercial, industrial, agricultural, institutional (i.e., public buildings such as schools), and recreational land uses are found in and around urban places. They are linked with one another by transportation. Often, planners use transportation lines to keep apart different land uses, such as housing and industry. Land-use maps can make communities better places to live.

Computer Application: Building a City

Some computer programs let you design your own city. For example, SIM CITY® starts with a computer-generated landscape. You pick the best site on which to build a community, and a year from 1900 to 2050. As you build your city, problems and disasters will occur. You will need to react wisely or spend tax money from the budget you have been given to try to solve these problems. SIM CITY® is as close as you can come to serving as mayor of a rapidly growing community.

FIGURE 1-25

SIM CITY® lets you investigate the ways in which communities develop.

10. Work with a partner to make a comparison chart of four communities. Decide upon the advantages and disadvantages on your own.

	Ouje'-Bougoumou, Quebec	Goderich, Ontario	Thompson, Manitoba	Vancouver, British Columbia
a) When was it surveyed?				
b) Who chose the plan?				
c) Describe the urban plan.				
d) Advantages of the plan.				
e) Disadvantages of the plan.				

11. Examine the topographic map in Figure 1–23.
    a) Describe the characteristics of the Canadian Shield evident on the map.
    b) How far is the mine site from the edge of town? List features that are found at the mine site.
    c) Make a list of community services shown on the map of Thompson (e.g., churches).
    d) Describe the pattern of the streets. How can you tell that Thompson is a planned community?

12. a) Why is it so important that frontier resource communities be pleasant places to live? Brainstorm a list of facilities and activities that would be important to include in planning a new northern town.
    b) Think of different ways to protect northern communities from becoming ghost towns when resources run low.

13. a) Use some of the concepts and examples from this chapter to make a plan of your own ideal community for about 500 to 1000 people. If you have a computer design program, such as SIM CITY®, work with it to design a large city instead.
    b) Use the urban land-use colours shown below to divide your map into land-use zones.
    c) Prepare a presentation or a report to explain the important ideas that are included in your design.

Common Colours for Land-Use Zones

Attached residential   Industrial

Detached residential   Parkland

Institutional   Forest

Commercial   Agricultural

PUTTING IT TOGETHER

1 Make a detailed land-use map of an area around your home, school, or nearby community. Start with a sketch-map on which you indicate the streets or roads in the study area. Then walk through the area, and make a rough copy map showing the different uses of the land.

2 Use the urban land-use colours above to make a neat, coloured copy of the land-use map. Include a legend and title.

3 What would you change in the map area to make your community a better place to live? Present your ideas in a report, display, or model.

PART 2

COMMUNITIES ARE PEOPLE

If you could live in any community in Canada, which would you choose? Some people might choose a big city or a warmer region. Others might be attracted to a scenic place in the mountains or by the sea. Many, however, would choose their own home town. There are strong personal connections and familiar experiences that go along with the places people know well.

This chapter will focus upon people. You will learn about city people and suburban populations. You will also see how people can have a voice in issues that affect their communities. Before you begin, decide whether or not each of these statements is true or false:

- Three-quarters of Canadians live in places with 1000 or more people.

- Three-quarters of Canadians live within a two-hour drive of the United States border.

- Three-quarters of Canadians live on .2 percent of Canada's total area.

- One-half of Canadians live in the Great Lakes-St. Lawrence Lowland.

- One-third of Canadians live in Metropolitan Toronto, Montreal, and Vancouver.

Check your answers on page 20.

Table 2–1 The five best big Canadian cities in which to live

In 1995, an international consulting firm ranked 120 world cities for "quality of life." Geneva, Switzerland, was rated first, but several Canadian cities also did very well.

Vancouver	2nd
Toronto	4th
Ottawa	6th
Montreal	7th
Calgary	11th

Key Words

- immigrant
- immigrant receiving areas
- cultural imprint
- suburbs
- bedroom community
- dormitory town
- blueprint
- official plan
- site plan

FIGURE 2–1

Left: Three-quarters of Canada's population is urban. Below: The rural population is largely resource-based, and includes Aboriginal hunters, farmers, miners, fishers, and loggers.

FIGURE 2–2

Have you ever been to any of these places? Would your own local community be a good candidate for the next list of best Canadian cities and towns?

- Best cities
- Best small cities and towns

Looking Forward

■ Why are new Canadians attracted to large metropolitan centres?

■ What factors can influence retired Canadians to move to a new community?

■ Where and why have commuter suburbs grown rapidly?

■ What sorts of "people places" have been created in our communities?

■ How are different members of the community involved in developing new projects?

Table 2–2 The ten best Canadian small cities and towns

In 1992, *Chatelaine* magazine reported its list of the ten safest, most affordable, and community-spirited places in Canada. They are listed below from east to west, with population figures.

Grand Falls-Windsor, Newfoundland (16 000)
Charlottetown, Prince Edward Island (16 800)
Truro, Nova Scotia (12 000)
Sussex, New Brunswick (4 200)
Kirkland, Quebec. (18 000)
Waterloo, Ontario (79 000)
Sarnia, Ontario (73 000)
Prince Albert, Saskatchewan (34 000)
Okotoks, Alberta (6 600)
Penticton, British Columbia (26 400)

People in the Community

A wide range of people can make up a community. Just think of the different types of students who make up the population of your school.

Across most of Canada, community populations can change a great deal in a very short time. For example, between 1986 and 1991, more than three-quarters of young adults and over one-quarter of seniors in Canada moved. Some people move within the community, but even more make a major relocation. Canadians are people on the move. In addition, Canada attracts about 200 000 new immigrants each year, most of them young adults. This section will examine two groups that have contributed to changes in various communities: immigrants and seniors.

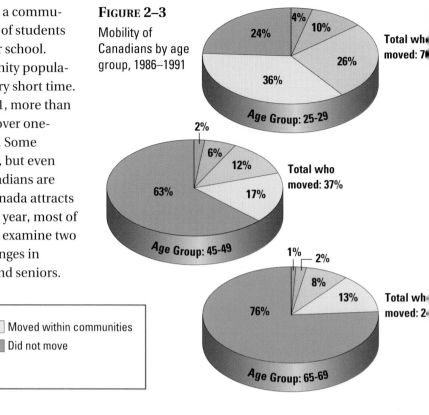

FIGURE 2–3

Mobility of Canadians by age group, 1986–1991

Total who moved: 7■
Age Group: 25-29
4% 10% 24% 26% 36%

Total who moved: 37%
Age Group: 45-49
2% 6% 12% 17% 63%

Total wh■ moved: 2■
Age Group: 65-69
1% 2% 8% 13% 76%

Legend:
- ▨ Moved between countries
- ▨ Moved between provinces
- ▨ Moved within provinces
- ▨ Moved within communities
- ▨ Did not move

Community Survey: People

1. Describe your own background. Include your age, birthplace, language, culture, and religion.

2. For each of the following questions, choose the best answer:
   - ■ **None**
   - ■ **A few**
   - ■ **Several**
   - ■ **Many**
   - ■ **Most**

   a) In your community or neighbourhood how many people are:
      i) Children?
      ii) Teenagers?
      iii) Adults?
      iv) Seniors?

   b) In your community or neighbourhood how many people are originally:
      i) From this region?
      ii) From other parts of Canada?
      iii) From other countries?

   c) In your community or neighbourhood how many people speak:
      i) English?
      ii) French?
      iii) English and French?
      iv) Other languages?

3. Which of the following are found in your neighbourhood or community? Give specific examples.
   a) Day-care centres for preschoolers
   b) Residences for seniors
   c) Places of worship
   d) Restaurants and stores reflecting a variety of cultures
   e) Clubs and organizations reflecting a variety of cultures

4. How, if at all, have the people in your neighbourhood or community changed in recent years?

Answers for page 18: The five statements are all true.

Today's Immigrants: Big City Bound

With the exception of Aboriginal peoples, Canada is a land of immigrants. Most of our ancestors came from other countries in the past. For the past 50 years, approximately one-sixth of Canada's population has been made up of immigrants. People who apply to immigrate to Canada must pass a rigorous "points test" based on education, language, job skills, and money for investment. Some new Canadians arrive as refugees, escaping political or military oppression.

FIGURE 2–4

Immigration to Canada: Top ten countries, 1981–1991

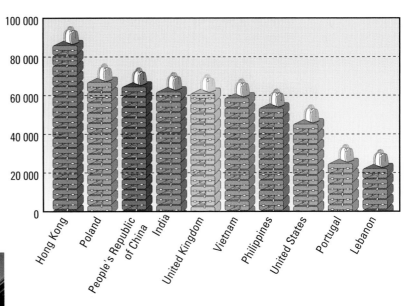

FIGURE 2–5

Canadian communities show the cultural imprint of a wide variety of peoples from around the world. Use these photos to explain the term "**cultural imprint**" and give some other examples.

Immigrants to Canada mainly settle west of Montreal. Three leading economic provinces, Ontario, British Columbia, and Alberta, are the most popular destinations, while French-speaking immigrants frequently select Quebec. Canada's metropolitan centres are especially attractive to immigrants. They offer important advantages such as jobs and business opportunities. In addition, large cities have **immigrant receiving areas**: neighbourhoods in which immigrants find familiar languages, places of worship, foods, and — most important — family or acquaintances.

Urban People: Thein Nguyen, Edmonton, Alberta

FIGURE 2–6
Thein Nguyen settled in Edmonton.

Thein Nguyen fled Communist Vietnam in an overcrowded boat in 1979. The converted fishing vessel anchored in Hong Kong harbour for weeks before it was permitted to land. Thein remained in a fenced refugee camp for almost two years before he was accepted to immigrate to Canada. He came to Edmonton where work was available in his trade. In Edmonton's Vietnamese community, Thein met and married May Van Tran. They have two children now and Thein is a machinist with a large firm serving the oil industry. The family owns a bungalow in Edmonton's east end.

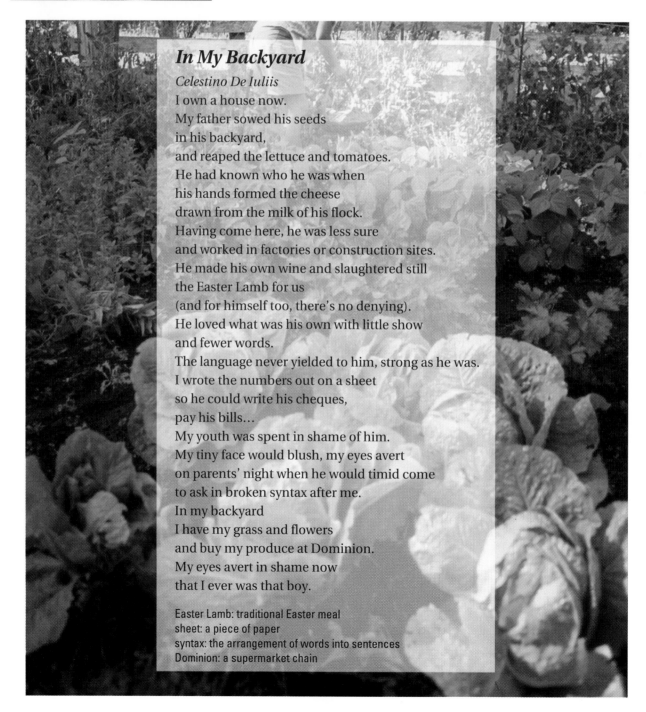

In My Backyard

Celestino De Iuliis

I own a house now.
My father sowed his seeds
in his backyard,
and reaped the lettuce and tomatoes.
He had known who he was when
his hands formed the cheese
drawn from the milk of his flock.
Having come here, he was less sure
and worked in factories or construction sites.
He made his own wine and slaughtered still
the Easter Lamb for us
(and for himself too, there's no denying).
He loved what was his own with little show
and fewer words.
The language never yielded to him, strong as he was.
I wrote the numbers out on a sheet
so he could write his cheques,
pay his bills…
My youth was spent in shame of him.
My tiny face would blush, my eyes avert
on parents' night when he would timid come
to ask in broken syntax after me.
In my backyard
I have my grass and flowers
and buy my produce at Dominion.
My eyes avert in shame now
that I ever was that boy.

Easter Lamb: traditional Easter meal
sheet: a piece of paper
syntax: the arrangement of words into sentences
Dominion: a supermarket chain

Seniors Wanted: Elliot Lake

Seniors are the Canadian group least likely to move. They usually have long-standing connections within their communities that they want to maintain. If seniors do move, it is often to be near other family members or to seek out a warmer retirement location. Elliot Lake, a fairly isolated mining town in Northern Ontario, seems an unlikely destination for older adults. Yet it is fast becoming one of Canada's most "senior" urban places. Chalk that up to some shrewd marketing by a small city in big trouble.

> ## Buyers Hit Gold at Elliot Lake
>
> Modern, spacious, well-built three-bedroom homes from $19 900, lot included. Join over 3000 seniors who have moved to Elliot Lake. Seeing is believing! For information, call…
>
> *Source: Active Living of Elliot Lake,* The Standard *newspaper, 1994.*

Table 2–3 Canadian communities by age group. Percentages show each community's population 65 and older.

Where seniors live in Canada Warm climates in southern Canada or rural areas that young people are leaving		Communities with younger populations Frontier resource towns or fast-growing urban areas	
Victoria, British Columbia	23.9%	Labrador City, Newfoundland	1.1%
Penticton, British Columbia	23.0%	Thompson, Manitoba	1.4%
Weyburn, Saskatchewan	22.5%	Pickering, Ontario	4.8%
Kelowna, British Columbia	19.1%	Calgary, Alberta	7.8%
St. Catharines, Ontario	15.0%	Edmonton, Alberta	8.5%

Many Canadian mining communities have become ghost towns, but Elliot Lake is determined not to be one of them. When uranium deposits were discovered, this community "boomed." By 1959, a modern new town had been built, offering all forms of housing — apartments, townhouses, duplexes, and detached homes. In that year, the population peaked at 25 000, but since then, Elliot Lake's numbers have varied with its uranium contracts. Two local mines closed in 1990, and another in 1992. By 1996, only one mine remained open and its last supply contract was to end in that year. At that time, the population of Elliot Lake was about 14 000.

Many of the modern homes in Elliot Lake had been left empty. As a result, these homes were cheap to buy or rent. Elliot Lake Retirement Living was first organized by the mining companies in 1987 to fill these empty homes. A massive television and newspaper advertising campaign has drawn thousands of seniors to visit the community each year. By 1996, some 5000 retirees had moved into the community. Elliot Lake will survive, perhaps with a greater proportion of seniors than almost any other Canadian community.

FIGURE 2–7

Location of Elliot Lake

FIGURE 2–8

Residential area, Elliot Lake, 1978. Note the site of a uranium mine in the background.

1. a) Use the information in this section to list five important conclusions about recent immigration to Canada.
    b) Outline reasons why immigrants today choose the destinations they do.

2. Reread the poem "In My Backyard."
    a) Find clues about the father's background. Where do you think he came from?
    b) Find clues about where the family lived in Canada. Why did they live there?
    c) Find clues that show immigration was difficult for the father. What was his biggest obstacle?
    d) How and why has the son's opinion of his father changed over the years?
    e) Why do you think the poet chose this title for the poem?

3. a) Reread the story of Thein Nguyen. Write the story about how and why your family came to the community and the home where you live now.
    b) Compare your story with the stories of others in the class. How are they similar or different?

4. Use an atlas and an outline map of Canada to mark the ten communities in Table 2–3. Use different colours for "old" and "young" populations. Describe and explain the patterns that you see.

5. a) Suggest reasons why Elliot Lake has targeted seniors instead of other groups.
    b) Make a list of the types of community services and activities Elliot Lake must provide for its senior population.
    c) In a chart, compare the benefits and disadvantages of living in Elliot Lake. Which types of seniors might enjoy it? Which might not?
    d) Discuss Elliot Lake with an older relative or friend. What is this person's opinion of moving there? Outline his or her reasons for responding in this way.

The Commuters: Suburban Growth

The cost of owning a home in Canada is high. Many people either rent apartments or houses. Nevertheless, more than half of all homes in Canada are detached houses, and most of these are owner-occupied. Only in the cities of Quebec are other dwelling types more popular. Elsewhere, people who can afford it often want the privacy and property that go with a detached home. This desire to own land has greatly affected the shape and area of many Canadian cities. It means that people will travel long distances to work if they can own property where it is less expensive — in the suburbs.

Suburbs are towns or residential areas outside the limit of a city. Many people live in the suburbs and commute to work. If most people in an area are commuters, the suburb is often called a **bedroom community** or **dormitory town**, suggesting that it is mostly a place to sleep between trips to work. Recent studies show that three-quarters of all trips to work are made by car. Bedroom communities have mainly detached houses, frequently with two motor vehicles in the driveway. High-speed expressways link most of these communities with the cities they rely on for employment. They are the fastest growing urban places in Canada.

Table 2–4 Summary of Canadian homes		
Average household size (number of persons)		2.67
Average number of rooms per dwelling		5.85
Owner-occupied households		63.3%
Mortgage-free owners		50.6%
Households by dwelling type	Single detached	57.0%
	Single attached	8.5%
	Apartment or flat	32.4%
	Mobile home	2.1%
Households in need of major repairs		10.0%

Source: Royal Bank Reporter, *Fall 1990/Ministry of Supply and Services,* Canada Year Book, 1994.

FIGURE 2–9

Many Canadian cities experienced suburban growth after the Second World War (1939–1945), when population grew rapidly. Bungalows built in the post-war period are found across the country.

The Growth of Suburbs

Compare the growth of suburbs and dormitory towns in two of Canada's largest urban areas. What connections can you see between the locations of these communities and transportation systems?

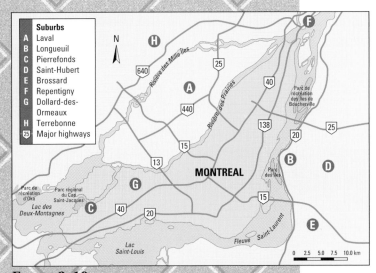

FIGURE 2–10
Metropolitan Montreal

Table 2–5 Population change in suburbs and bedroom communities in the Montreal area

	1966	1981	1991
Laval	196 100	268 300	319 400
Longueuil	25 600	124 300	129 900
Pierrefonds	27 924	38 400	78 700
Saint-Hubert	17 200	60 600	74 000
Brossard	11 900	52 200	64 800
Repentigny	14 976	34 400	49 600
Dollard-des-Ormeaux	12 297	39 900	46 900
Terrebonne	7 480	11 800	39 700

Table 2–6 Population change in suburbs and bedroom communities in the Vancouver area

	1966	1981	1991
Surrey	81 800	147 100	245 200
Richmond	50 500	96 100	126 600
Coquitlam/Port Coquitlam	11 121	88 600	120 800
Delta	20 700	74 700	89 000
North Vancouver	48 100	65 400	75 200
Matsqui	16 200	42 000	68 100
Chilliwack	8 681	31 522	51 000
Maple Ridge (Haney)	2 800	22 145	50 000

FIGURE 2–11
Metropolitan Vancouver

Urban People: Christine Gaigal, Hamilton, Ontario

FIGURE 2–12

Christine Gaigal

Christine Gaigal is a dental assistant who commutes to her job in central Toronto. Over the years, she has travelled to work from Richmond Hill in the north, from Peterborough in the east, and from Hamilton in the west. When she lived in Peterborough, she had to leave home at 5:00 a.m., and drive for an hour and a half to reach Toronto.

When Christine and her husband moved to Hamilton, to be closer to his work, she had another commuting option. Their home is a short drive from the local GoBus service. She can board the bus at Hamilton, sleep for half an hour on the highway to Toronto, and then catch the subway to the office. Three different transportation systems work better than the one she relied on when she lived in Peterborough.

FIGURE 2–13

These photographs show the same location in Scarborough, now part of Metropolitan Toronto, in 1956 and 1973. Identify the changes that took place.

People Places in the Heart of the City

FIGURE 2–14

Stanley Park, a peninsula adjacent to Vancouver's city core, is one of the largest forested areas within a Canadian city. It was preserved as parkland very early in Vancouver's history.

The city centre can be a forlorn and even dangerous spot, or it can be alive with people. Many Canadian communities have used progressive ideas to create "people places" downtown, to bring people into the heart of the city.

Often communities contain green spaces within them, parks that were set aside early in the community's history. A more recent trend has brought other types of "people places" to the centre of many Canadian cities. Exciting new recreational areas have been established where old factories, warehouses, canals, and railway yards once stood.

The Old Port of Montreal

This superb two-kilometre site offers a host of activities, quality entertainment, and exciting excursions.

- Imax 3D: The pictures are so real you can almost touch them....

- La Balade: A bilingual guided tour introducing the history of the Old Port....

- The Flea Market: You can browse for hours through more than 100 stands with 1001 treasures!

- Bonsecours Stage: A wide range of free activities on an outdoor stage....

- Restaurants and picnic areas.

- The Port d'Escale: This harbour offers owners of pleasure craft 95 berths with electricity, water and sanitation services.

Source: Old Port of Montréal Corporation: Montreal Tourist Guide

FIGURE 2–15

In Halifax, Quebec City, Montreal, Toronto, Vancouver, and other communities, little-used port areas have been recycled into waterfront parks, such as the "Old Port of Montreal."

Community Survey: People Places

1. Which of the following recreation areas are located in your community? Which are located in another community within a 15-minute drive?
   a) Playground for children
   b) Baseball diamond
   c) Soccer or football field
   d) Paved outdoor basketball area
   e) Golf course
   f) Outdoor community swimming area
   g) Indoor community pool
   h) Community skating area
   i) Indoor rink for hockey, skating
   j) Indoor curling rink

2. Which of the following relaxation areas are located in your community? Which are located within a 15-minute drive?
   a) A park to relax in
   b) A wooded parkland with trails
   c) A good area for a picnic
   d) A place for boating or fishing
   e) Trails for cross-country skiing
   f) Trails for winter snowmobiling
   g) A place for fireworks displays
   h) A place for community parades

3. Which of the following gathering places are located in your community? Which are located within a 15-minute drive?
   a) An indoor shopping mall
   b) A gym for after-school activities
   c) A public square or monument
   d) A place of worship
   e) A public market (e.g., farmer's market)
   f) A public auditorium
   g) A public library
   h) Exhibition grounds or fairground

4. Which items from the lists above should be added to your community? Why?

FIGURE 2–16

Why is a shopping mall a popular gathering spot for young people?

The Forks: Winnipeg's People Place

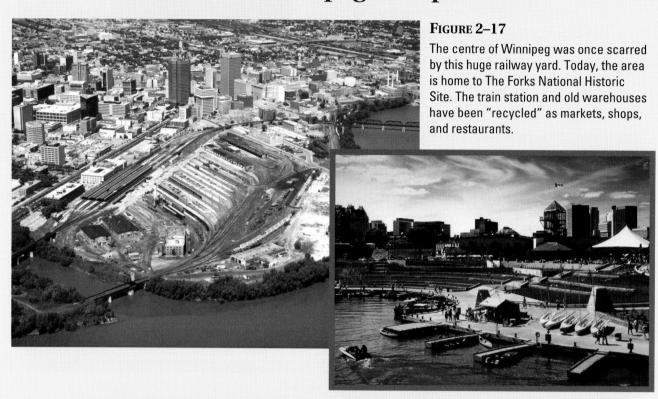

FIGURE 2–17

The centre of Winnipeg was once scarred by this huge railway yard. Today, the area is home to The Forks National Historic Site. The train station and old warehouses have been "recycled" as markets, shops, and restaurants.

FIGURE 2–18

The Forks is now a "fun" place in the old city centre. Match these maps to the photographs above.

6. Work with a partner. One of you should examine the information for Montreal and the other should examine the information for Vancouver (page 25). For each city:
   a) Calculate the total number of people living in all eight suburbs in 1966, 1981, and 1991.
   b) Identify which four suburbs grew most
      i) between 1966 and 1981
      ii) between 1981 and 1991
   c) Examine the location of these suburbs on the map. How far are they from the city centre? Compare the locations of the suburbs that grew rapidly *before* 1981 and those that grew *after* 1981.
   d) Compare your results with those of your partner. What similarities and differences can you find between the two big centres?

7. a) Plan and conduct a traffic survey at busy intersections in your neighbourhood or community. Count vehicles travelling in different directions for 6 minutes (x 10 = hourly flow).
   b) Prepare graphs and flow maps of your findings. Use them to identify problems with traffic flow.

c) Recommend solutions to any traffic problems you identified in your survey.

8. a) Compare the new people places that have been created in downtown Montreal and Winnipeg. What similarities do you see?
   b) Brainstorm a list of good effects that such places can have on a downtown area. Consider the viewpoints of downtown residents, merchants, suburban residents, tourists, and others.

9. a) Make an inventory of the parks and public places in your community, starting with the largest area. List the activities that are available at each of these places. List the special events held there.
   b) Suggest improvements that could be made in the parks and public places of your community. What recreational activities does your community still need?

10. Does your community need facilities for people who are homeless (shelters, drop-in centres, etc.)? Investigate what facilities, if any, exist. Where are they located? Are they adequate? Prepare a report of your findings.

People and Development in the Community

Every community has vacant land. Perhaps the land hasn't been used since a factory or railway yard closed. Perhaps the property was never built upon at all. In most cases, communities see vacant land as a resource to use wisely.

Developing vacant land brings together citizens, local government, people with professional expertise, and **entrepreneurs** — business investors who believe they can make a profit from a new or renovated building at that location.

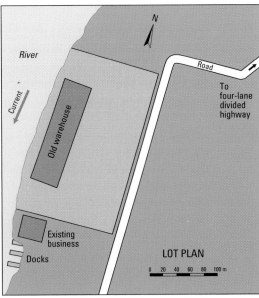

FIGURE 2–19

Vacant lands are sites available for new uses. Sometimes old buildings on vacant land can be used for new purposes.

New and renovated buildings are designed by **architects.** They prepare a **blueprint**, a type of map that shows how space is to be used inside the building. They must also prepare a detailed **site plan**. This is a map that details how a property will be used. If, for example, the new property is a hotel, the site plan would outline the building itself, driveways and walks, parking, and outdoor areas such as pools and patios, trees, and signs.

Each new project must be approved by the local government. To get approval, the project must fit the community's **official plan**, a detailed land-use map that sets out the legal use of all property in the community. The official plan directs the pattern of growth in the community, and prevents the mixing of incompatible land uses such as heavy industry and housing.

If the project is approved, land surveyors are brought in to measure the property boundaries and translate the details of the site plan onto the property before construction begins.

Career Profile: Rose Britton, Professional Land Surveyor

Rose Britton has had 16 years' experience in all aspects of land surveying. She has carried out surveys in four provinces and is currently Division Manager with a major Alberta survey firm.

Rose's present work involves site inspections, cost estimates, and overall management of survey projects.

"Most surveyors work to set boundaries for parcels of land. This includes subdividing land for housing and laying out highway right-of-ways.

"Traditional survey crews used several people to operate the survey instrument (or theodolite), an elevation rod, and a long measuring chain. Today, two-person crews are more common. We use an electronic instrument that flashes an electronic beam to reflect back from a glass prism. The survey chain is becoming a thing of the past."

Several Canadian universities offer a four-year degree in surveying through the faculties of geography, science, and engineering. Technological survey programs lasting from one to three years are available at many colleges. Many Canadian women and men enjoy professional careers as land surveyors.

FIGURE 2–20
Student surveyors at work

Activities

11. a) Imagine that you are planning a new hotel. What sort of hotel would you like to stay in for a weekend? What sort of hotel is most likely to succeed? How could it attract tourists, banquets, and business conventions?

    b) Make a list of all the services you would provide in a major hotel for travellers and conventions; for example, suites, pools, etc.

    c) Draw and title a full-page sketch of the front of your hotel on a blank sheet of paper. Make it "wheelchair friendly."

    d) Use a ruler to make a full-page blueprint of the main-floor level of your hotel.

12. a) Use a full page of blank paper to make a neat outline of the vacant lot in Figure 2–19.

    b) On this lot, use a ruler to make a detailed site plan for your hotel. Don't let the hotel building cover more than half of the lot. Use the rest for parking, landscaping, signs, outdoor areas, and so on.

13. Use your completed hotel front view, blueprint, and site plan to prepare a report to community officials asking for a building permit.

    a) Highlight the main characteristics of your designs and plans in a positive way.

    b) Convince the officials that you have used the lot wisely to create something of benefit to the whole community.

What happens when the parties involved in land development in a community don't agree? For example, suppose that local residents in the neighbourhood where your ideal hotel is to be built are opposed to the plans. The local government is refusing to issue a building permit until an agreement is reached between local people and the developers. How can the problem be solved? One tool that can help work out disagreements is the problem-solving wheel shown below.

1 Look closely at the illustrations around the diagram of the problem-solving wheel. They show what happened when local residents opposed the plan for the hotel. Use the problem-solving wheel as a guide to re-arrange the story in order.

2 Give your opinion of the solution. Is it fair? Why or why not?

3 Apply the following problem-solving wheel to an issue that is important in your community at present.

FIGURE 2–21   Solving community issues: The problem-solving wheel

PART 3

CANADIAN CITY ISSUES

Chronic Water Shortage Empties Reservoir

ABC services folds: 50 jobs lost

Report warns of housing shortage

Council Undecided on Community Arena

Coliform counts close city beaches

FIGURE 3–1
News headlines: Typical types of community issues

Community issues are always in the news. Headlines such as the ones shown here often tell us about issues that can affect our health, our incomes, and our satisfaction with community life. Finding solutions to such issues is not the responsibility of politicians alone. The opinions and participation of citizens are often a very important part of decisions that affect the community.

This chapter examines social, political, and environmental questions in three Canadian cities, and invites you to investigate similar issues in your own area. Urban renewal in Halifax, public transit in Toronto, and environmental quality in Vancouver are serious issues for all community members. What are your views?

Before you begin this chapter, examine the information on these two pages and answer the following questions:

■ Look at the news headlines in Figure 3–1. Have any similar issues emerged where you live?

■ Name some other important issues or problems your community faces at present.

■ Is it better to replace run-down neighbourhoods with new apartment blocks or to upgrade existing homes?

■ Does your community offer different forms of public transportation to reduce the use of automobiles?

■ Does your community pollute local waters, air, or land areas?

Key Words

◆ census tract
◆ urban renewal
◆ Census Metropolitan Area (CMA)
◆ municipality
◆ infrastructure
◆ public transit
◆ intensive agriculture
◆ extensive agriculture

FIGURE 3-2

Vancouver's SkyTrain. Public transit is expensive. Could higher gasoline taxes be used to pay for it? Would more expensive gas encourage drivers to use public transit instead? What would be the benefit for the environment?

FIGURE 3-3

In the 1960s, many cities demolished run-down neighbourhoods and replaced them with new housing complexes. Planners today question this approach to urban renewal.

FIGURE 3-4

Waste disposal has become a major urban environmental problem. Outlying communities do not want to become sites for urban garbage exports.

Looking Forward

■ How can Census of Canada information be used to compare city neighbourhoods?

■ What should be done about run-down neighbourhoods?

■ What problems develop when a city keeps growing beyond its political boundaries?

■ How can maps and air photographs be used to plan the growth of a large city?

■ Will environmental problems ruin the quality of life in the lower Fraser valley?

Social Issue: Neighbourhoods in Downtown Halifax

Halifax has always been a port city. The sheltered channel leading into Bedford Basin gives it one of the largest deep-water harbours in the world. The site was occupied by the Micmac First Nation before the British brought 2500 settlers to the location in 1749. Early economic growth was based on the export of fish and lumber to the West Indies and Britain. During the past century, Halifax has become the Atlantic region's major centre for government institutions, education, transportation, and product distribution.

The navy and armed forces have always been important in the Halifax economy, but during the First World War, their presence nearly destroyed the city. In 1917, two ships collided in The Narrows between Halifax and nearby Dartmouth. One vessel was loaded with explosives. The explosion that followed was the biggest unnatural blast in history, until the atomic bomb was developed. Its effects are still seen today in the characteristics of Halifax's neighbourhoods.

FIGURE 3–5

The Central Business District of Halifax from the harbour. Citadel Hill, the fortress overlooking the city, is partly visible behind these new office towers.

FIGURE 3–6

Halifax after the 1917 explosion

Amazing Facts About the Halifax Explosion

- 2.5 million kilograms of explosives blew 1.5 kilometres high.
- 2.5 square kilometres — half of Halifax — was levelled.
- 16 000 buildings were destroyed and 12 000 others damaged.
- 20 percent of Halifax's population was killed or injured.
- 200 people were permanently blinded by flying glass.
- 100 kilometres away windows were shattered by the shock.

Halifax occupies a hilly peninsula between the harbour and an inlet called the Northwest Arm. The aerial photograph in Figure 3–7 shows wharves and commercial buildings lining the harbourfront. North of the star-shaped Citadel fortress and behind the harbour is a neighbourhood known as the North End. It was destroyed and rebuilt after the Halifax Explosion. The area south of the Citadel fortress was largely protected from the blast by distance and the terrain. This historic South End neighbourhood reaches over to the Northwest Arm.

Data from the Census of Canada can be used to compare the characteristics of Halifax's North End and South End neighbourhoods. A **census** is a detailed recording of population and economic information. The first detailed census of Canada East and West was collected in 1851. Since then, a census has been held every ten years. In 1956, the first "mini-census" was conducted to provide accurate population data halfway between the major recording dates. Table 3–1 (page 36) uses some of the hundreds of different types of facts collected in 1991 to compare two **census tract**s near the core of Halifax.

FIGURE 3–7
Aerial photograph of South Halifax

1. Analyze the photograph above. Find the following:
   a) Waterfront features:
      i) Large waterfront warehouses
      ii) small wharves and ships
      iii) high-rise buildings along the harbour
   b) Land-use features:
      i) Halifax Citadel (fort overlooking the city)
      ii) Island Garrison (protected harbour entry)
      iii) Central Business District (tallest buildings)
      iv) Forested South End neighbourhood

   c) Transportation features:
      i) Railway terminal
      ii) Large ship being loaded
      iii) Expressways leading to downtown
      iv) Grid pattern of streets

2. Compare Figures 3–5 and 3–7.
   a) Which specific features can be seen in both photographs?
   b) From which point in Figure 3–7 was the photograph in Figure 3–5 taken?

POPULATION ORIGINS

Information	South End Tract 005	North End Tract 010
1. Population, 1991	1 918	5 746
2. Mobility, 1986–1991		
a) Moved since 1986	730	3 275
b) Did not move	1 100	1 630
3. Immigrant population		
a) To Canada before 1961	50	75
b) To Canada 1961–1981	250	130
c) To Canada 1981–1991	40	385
4. Ethnic origins		
a) Multiple origins	800	1 670
b) British ancestry	805	1 830
c) Other European	15	415
d) Aboriginal	0	60
e) Black ancestry	0	1 040
f) Other ancestries	310	605

ECONOMIC CHARACTERISTICS

Information	South End Tract 005	North End Tract 010
1. Population, 1991	1 918	5 746
2. Education completed (ages 15+)		
a) less than Grade 9	0	960
b) Grade 9 to 13	240	1 570
c) Skilled trade/Other education	180	910
d) Some university education	235	525
e) University degree	905	625
3. Job categories		
a) Management, professions	805	775
b) Sales and services	285	1 605
c) Machinery, transport, construction	30	245
d) Other employment	15	105

FAMILY HOUSING CHARACTERISTICS

Information	South End Tract 005	North End Tract 010
1. Income levels		
a) Family average	$125 207	$25 164
b) Low income families	3.9%	44.3%
2. Home ownership		
a) Family owns their home	400	155
b) Average home value	$300 958	$94 194
c) Family rents their home	75	760
d) Average rent per month	$859	$507
e) Homes need major repair	30	245
3. Types of dwellings		
a) Single detached houses	520	140
b) Semi-detached houses	10	140
c) Townhouses, row houses	5	365
d) Apartments, detached duplex	20	130
e) Apartment building units	110	1 625
f) Other homes	0	30

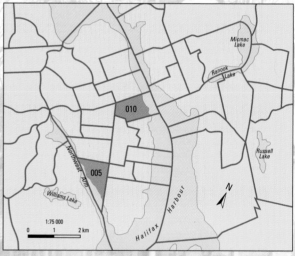

FIGURE 3–8

Census tracts in the core area of Halifax

There are great social and economic contrasts among Halifax's older areas. The South End has long been a centre for higher education. There are three universities there: Dalhousie, St. Mary's, and the University of King's College. As a result, many well-educated, high-income professionals live in the area. Many of the large homes in the South End were built before the Halifax Explosion, but survived the blast.

The North End is near the harbour and has a long history as a working-class district. Rents and house prices are quite low, making the area attractive to new immigrants and low-income families. Much of Halifax's Black population — mostly descendants of Loyalists who left America after the Revolutionary War — live in the North End. Many have been there since the city bulldozed their nearby community, Africville, in the 1960s.

Urban Renewal in Halifax's Africville

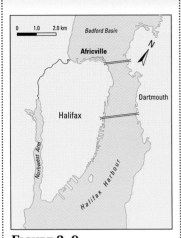

FIGURE 3–9
Location of Africville

FIGURE 3–10
Trains ran through the centre of Africville. What problems would they have caused?

1783
- 2500 Black Loyalists arrive in Nova Scotia after the American Revolution.

1848
- A small Black community, to become known as Africville, established north of Halifax on Bedford Bay.

1878
- Africville has 20 homes, a church, and a school.

1910
- Land surrounding Africville used by the growing city of Halifax for railroads, industries, a slaughterhouse, sewage disposal, a garbage dump, a prison, and a hospital for infectious diseases.

1930s
- Africville residents succeed in getting a post office and street lights from the City of Halifax, but no water or sewer services.

1948, 1959
- Surveys show that about two-thirds of Africville's residents want to stay, but with improved services for the community.

1962
- City of Halifax calculates it will cost $800 000 to upgrade Africville; recommends demolition instead.

1964
- First relocation of Africville residents; city buys Africville homes for $500 each.

1970
- Demolition of last home in Africville. Total cost of removing the community reaches $765 000, ten times the original estimate.

"Why did people agree to leave Africville?... They tried in so many ways to get little improvements. They tried for ordinary services and they failed."

Source: Africville Steering Committee, The Spirit of Africville (Halifax: Maritext, 1992), p. 47.

FIGURE 3–11
Many families from Africville relocated in Uniacke Square, in Halifax's North End.

Survey of Former Africville Residents

1. Do you miss Africville life?
   - Very much: 73%
   - Some: 7%
   - Little or none: 17%
   - No response: 3%

2. Do you have contact with former close friends from Africville?
   - Regular contact: 53%
   - Reduced contact: 20%
   - Little contact: 27%

3. What problems were brought by relocation?
   - Money worries: 72%
   - Household worries: 40%
   - Marital strains: 17%
   - Job problems: 16%

Source: Donald H. Clairmont and Dennis William Magill, Africville: The Life and Death of a Canadian Black Community (Toronto: McClelland and Stewart, 1974), pp. 222–231.

Many Canadian communities have undertaken **urban renewal** projects in deteriorating neighbourhoods. The Forks in Winnipeg and the Old City of Montreal are examples of areas where the old has been blended with the new. In many cities, however, bulldozers have torn down old areas so that completely new developments could be built. In doing so, they have destroyed a sense of community that was very important to inhabitants. How do you think urban renewal of a neighbourhood should best be handled?

Problem: A neighbourhood is physically substandard, and the residents are not well-off. Community members are calling for urban renewal of the area.

Options:

1. Accept that communities have many types of neighbourhoods. Leave the situation as it is.
2. Keep the buildings, but spend public and private money to upgrade housing and other facilities.
3. Demolish all substandard dwellings and replace them with new rental units.
4. Help the residents to move elsewhere, then develop the area for other uses such as industry, parkland, or offices.

Which option offers the best approach to urban renewal? Use the problem-solving wheel to reach a decision.

Activities

1. Imagine that you are a newspaper reporter in 1917. Write an exciting headline and news report about the Halifax Explosion. Before you begin, look for more information on the explosion in other books and on CD-ROM.

2. a) Use Figures 3–5 and 3–7 to identify advantages of Halifax's site.
   b) Compare Halifax's site with that of Vancouver in Figure 3–21 (page 44).

3. Work in a small group. Divide Table 3–1 among your group members.
   a) Examine your section of information and list important similarities and differences that you can see between the South End and the North End. Note that Census Tract 010 has three times more people.
   b) Prepare graphs to show the most important findings in your section of the table.
   c) Meet as a group to compare your findings. What are the major differences between the two neighbourhoods? Are there important similarities? Find reasons in the text for the characteristics of the two neighbourhoods.
   d) Why would a community planner find census information useful? What other types of information would be needed before making changes in a neighbourhood? Why?

4. Discuss the case of Africville. Was it a good idea to demolish the neighbourhood? Would other options have been effective? Do you think racist attitudes may have influenced decisions that were made? Explain your views.

5. Discuss the problem-solving question of urban renewal with a small group.
   a) What are the advantages and disadvantages of each of the four options identified? Are there other possible solutions that you can add? Prepare a large chart of your findings.
   b) Decide on the solution that you favour. Outline your reasons either in a group presentation or an individual letter to the mayor.

6. How would an urban renewal decision be made in your community? Identify:
   a) Municipal government: Who are your representatives?
   b) Citizens groups: Which groups represent different neighbourhoods or interests in the community (school associations, recycling committee, etc.)?
   c) Business groups: Which business associations are influential in the community (Chamber of Commerce, etc.)?
   d) Others: Who else would have an influential voice in decisions made where you live?

Political Issue: Providing Services in the Toronto Region

Is Canada's biggest city Montreal or Toronto? In a way, neither one is. Edmonton covers the largest metropolitan area in Canada. In terms of population, however, Metropolitan Toronto is Canada's largest city.

Census Canada measures the area and population of large cities using **Census Metropolitan Areas (CMAs)**. A CMA includes both the large city and the area beyond it where at least half the people who live there work in the city. In Edmonton's case, the CMA covers an area of about 10 000 km^2, almost double Toronto's area. Toronto's CMA, however, had about 4 million people in 1991, close to the combined population of six provinces and the northern territories! Toronto's population has constantly spilled over the city's boundaries. The city, with a fairly small population of 10 000 people, became the provincial capital in 1834. By 1912, it had annexed 7 nearby communities and grown to 375 000. By 1953, there were 675 000 Torontonians and another 450 000 people living nearby in the surrounding suburbs. There were many problems.

Canada's first regional government, the Government of Metropolitan Toronto, was formed in 1953 to deal with problems of growth. This level of government began to plan the network of transportation, water, parkland, and other basic services for the city and surrounding areas. Meanwhile, local governments, or **municipalities**, continued to manage their own community services such as streets, local parks, and libraries.

The Toronto area has continued to grow rapidly since 1953. Regional governments were set up all around Metro Toronto, in an area that planners now call the Greater Toronto Area (GTA). As the GTA grows, the task of planning its infrastructure becomes more difficult. **Infrastructure** refers to the network of roads, schools, and other services that support the area. Many different communities and elected officials must cooperate if a metropolitan area is to function smoothly. It has been suggested that a new, single "supercity" level of government be set up to organize the GTA.

Suburb Problems in Toronto, about 1950

- he suburbs could not afford to ovide services because they d few industries or businesses tax.
- he suburbs relied on local wells, they faced water shortages.
- adequate suburban sewage eatment plants were polluting cal rivers.
- ttle open parkland was being t aside between the suburbs.
- burban commuters relied on private bus and rail systems, with their own fare systems.

FIGURE 3–12
Toronto waterfront, 1834, looking west from the Don River

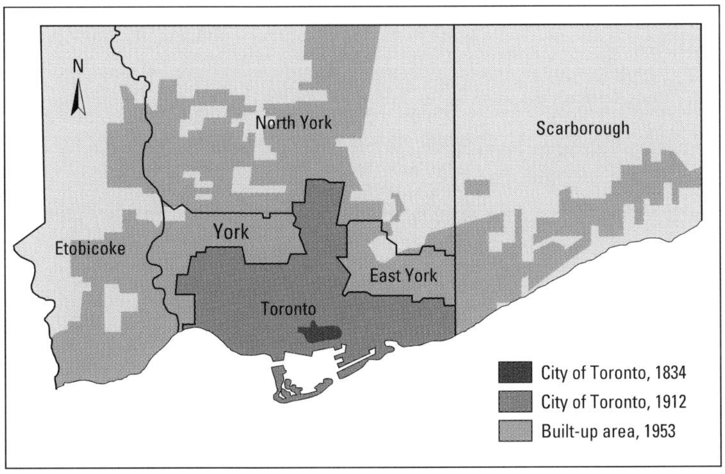

FIGURE 3–13
Growth of Toronto, 1834–1953

Map legend:
- City of Toronto, 1834
- City of Toronto, 1912
- Built-up area, 1953

FIGURE 3–14
Toronto waterfront, 1894, looking east along the railway lines

Getting Around the GTA

A Transportation Profile

In 1992, a publishing company in Metro Toronto conducted a survey of its employees' transportation patterns to work. All employees worked in Scarborough, the northeastern part of Metro Toronto, but they lived all over the Greater Toronto Area. The office is very close to three expressways: Highway 401, Highway 404, and the Don Valley Parkway (DVP). Regular bus service also connects the workplace to other parts of Metro Toronto. The results of the transportation survey of 191 employees are shown in Table 3–2.

Table 3–2 Home communities of Scarborough office employees

City of Scarborough	95
City of Toronto	34
City of North York	19
All Others	43:
Pickering	9
Ajax	8
Markham	5
Oshawa	4
Whitby	4
Vaughan	3
Richmond Hill	3
Stouffville	2
Hamilton	1
Port Hope	1
Uxbridge	1
Mississauga	1
Hastings County	1
Total	191

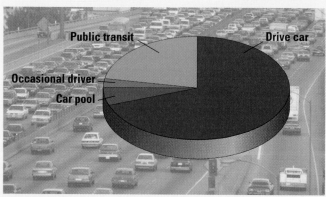

FIGURE 3–15

Employees' methods of transportation to Scarborough office

FIGURE 3–16

Communities and major highways in the Metro Toronto Area

Public Transit in the GTA

Getting around the GTA can be very difficult. Figure 3–18 shows that tremendous amounts of traffic flow along routes to and from Metropolitan Toronto. The major east-west corridor, Highway 401, is 12 lanes wide, but it still clogs up during rush-hour. **Public transit** — buses, subways, streetcars, and trains — provides an alternative to private vehicles. The Toronto transit service, the TTC, is heavily used within Metro Toronto.

Outside Metro, commuters have to pay twice (or more) if they change buses to cross regional boundaries. For example, a public-transit trip from suburban Richmond Hill to downtown Toronto requires one fare for Richmond Hill Transit and another for the TTC. Furthermore, the journey could require two transfers (bus to bus to subway). Although there were 14 million "cross-border" transit trips in 1991, many suburban commuters prefer to drive.

Some planners have suggested a single-fare system in which commuters could travel between transit regions on the same ticket. This system would reduce fares and encourage more suburban commuters to use transit. However, commuters would still have to transfer between different systems. In addition, lower fares would mean less money for the governments that fund public transportation. Some have proposed a special gasoline tax in the GTA, which would help pay for transit systems and encourage more drivers to use public transportation.

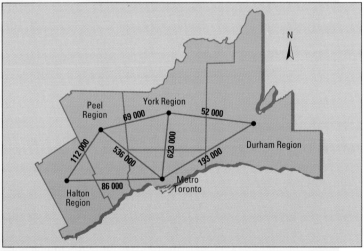

Using the Problem-Solving Wheel: Transit in the GTA

Problem: It is difficult and expensive to get around the Greater Toronto Area.

Options:

1. Leave the situation as it is: congested highways; a two-fare transit system; planning divided among several different municipalities.
2. Build more highways, if there is agreement among the different regional governments, and accept the environmental consequences of increased automobile use.
3. Encourage more commuters to use transit by having a single-fare system paid for by a gasoline tax, if the different municipalities will agree to it.
4. Create a new level of regional government for the whole GTA to operate a single, "seamless" region-wide transit system and other basic public services.

Which option offers the best solution for the transportation problems faced by the Greater Toronto Area? Use the problem-solving wheel to reach a decision.

FIGURE 3–17

Toronto waterfront and skyline in 1995

FIGURE 3–18

Number of daily trips between communities in the Toronto region, 1991. Identify the three most numerous trips on this map. Suggest reasons for this pattern.

Community Survey: Private Transportation and Public Transit

1. Does your family have any motor vehicles? If so, how many?

2. Which forms of public transit are available in your community?
   a) School buses
   b) Bus service
   c) Mini-buses for seniors, the disabled
   d) Subways, commuter rail service
   e) Other (specify)

3. Choose from these transportation types to answer the following questions:
   - On foot
   - By bike
   - By school bus
   - By car
   - By bus/subway
   - Other (specify)

   a) How do you normally travel to school?
   b) How do you normally get to recreational activities?
   c) How do adults at home normally travel to work? (Specify for each adult.)

   d) How do they get to where they shop? (Specify whether they shop downtown or at a shopping centre.)

4. Compare the use of private vehicles and public transportation in the community. What are the advantages and disadvantages of each?

5. Find out:
   a) If you have any family vehicles, how many total kilometres do they travel each year? Canadians average about 6000 km per licensed driver per year. How does your family compare?
   b) Does your family spend more, less, or the same as the Canadian average of about one-eighth of the family budget on transportation? What are the costs of owning a car?

Activities

7. a) Compare the Toronto area in 1834, 1912, 1953, and 1991 in terms of:
   - the total population
   - the size of the built up area (in kilometres)
   - the compass direction of growth of the built-up area

   b) Compare the pictures of the Toronto waterfront in 1834, 1894, and 1995 in terms of:
   - types of buildings visible
   - types of transportation visible
   - public access to the waterfront

8. a) Explain the following terms in your notebook:

CMA	municipality
GTA	infrastructure
transit	regional planning

   b) Explain how metropolitan government operates.

9. a) Locate the office of the Scarborough publishing company on the map in Figure 3–16. Identify the expressway systems on the map that could be used by those who drive to work.

   b) Use Figure 3–15 to identify what fraction of the office employees arrive by car.

10. a) Brainstorm two lists to show the advantages and disadvantages of living in a large metropolitan area.

    b) Imagine that your family is moving to, or away from, a large Canadian city. Write a letter to a friend telling how you feel about the decision.

11. Complete the Transportation Survey. Compile the results for the class and prepare charts and graphs of the data. Use a computer spreadsheet and graphics program, if possible.

12. Make a map of your neighbourhood or community to show your typical routes and forms of transportation from home to each of the following destinations. Use different colours for each.
    a) to school
    b) to a favourite recreation place
    c) to a shopping area (or downtown)
    d) to a few friends' homes

13. a) Evaluate the four options for the future of transportation in the GTA (page 41).
    b) Hold a public meeting where speakers explain their favoured solution.
    c) As a class, try to agree on one solution.

Environmental Issue: Vancouver's Impact

Aboriginal peoples lived in the area of Vancouver at least 2000 years ago, but the present city is just over a century old. In 1886, Burrard Inlet was chosen as the western end of the trans-continental railway line. Growth was rapid. By 1900, Vancouver had become British Columbia's leading commercial centre. By the 1960s, it was Canada's leading port, and by 1971, the metropolitan area population reached 1 million. There will be 2 million Vancouverites early in the twenty-first century. The metropolitan Vancouver area is one of the fastest growing regions in Canada.

FIGURE 3–19

Vancouver has one of the most beautiful city locations in the world, with its well-protected deep-water harbour on Burrard Inlet backing up against the snow-capped Coast Ranges.

FIGURE 3–20

Population increase of Metropolitan Vancouver, 1951–2011
(Data for 2011 projected by B.C. Ministry of Finance)

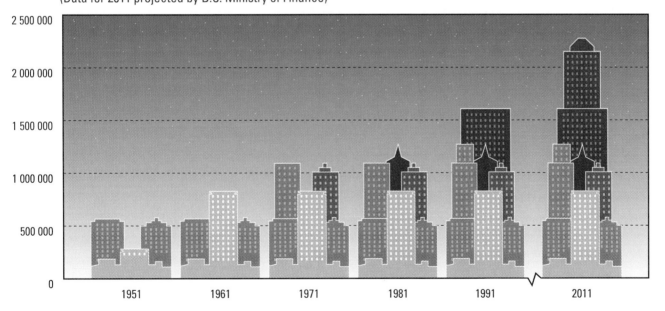

Vancouver's direct influence has extended far up the Fraser River valley. The city's housing prices are by far the highest in Canada, leading many people to commute long distances. For example, about 100 000 people live in the Matsqui and Abbotsford area, 65 km upstream from Vancouver. More than 50 000 live in the Chilliwack district, 100 km up the Fraser from the city. Chilliwack's location on the Trans-Canada Highway makes it increasingly attractive to commuters willing to make a two- to three-hour round-trip to work each day.

FIGURE 3-21

Lower Fraser Valley. Scale: 1:250 000 (1 cm = 2.5 km). There is little space for expansion in British Columbia's lower mainland area; therefore, urban development has spilled into the fertile farmlands of the Fraser River delta and valley.

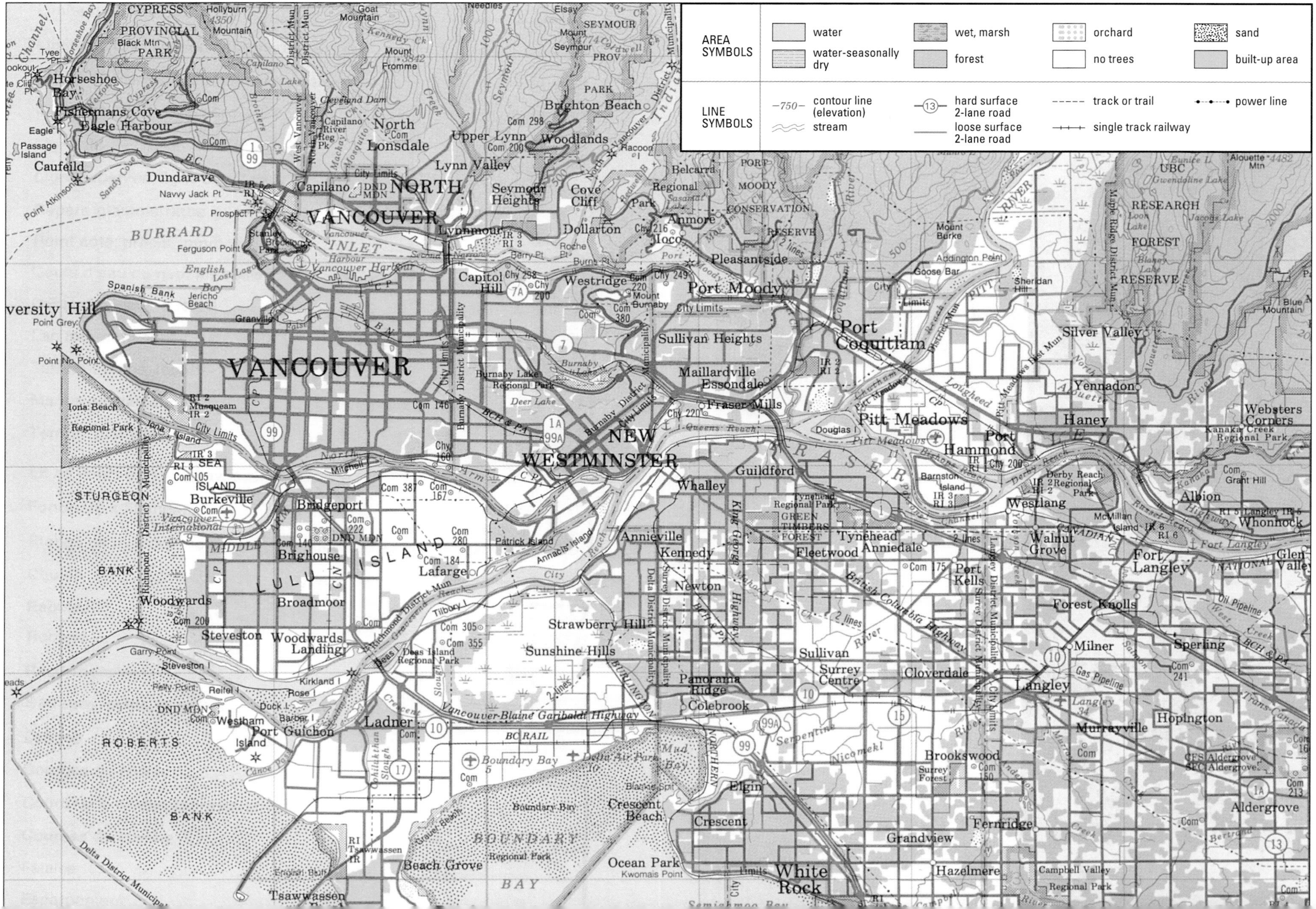

Urban Growth and Habitat Destruction

The rapid growth of Vancouver has created many environmental problems. In the delta area near the mouth of the Fraser, only about one-eighth of the land remains in a natural state. A river delta is usually a flat, marshy area of meadows and bogs, ideal habitat for birds and small animals. During the mild winter months, the lower mainland area has the highest densities of waterfowl and shore birds in Canada. However, land drainage and flood control measures have caused a sharp drop in many species.

Fish populations of the lower Fraser River have also been affected by habitat change. Community sewage disposal, industrial discharges, and farm run-off threaten species such as trout and sturgeon. The serious decline in salmon stocks in the 1990s can be blamed on both overfishing and loss of habitat.

Fraser River Pollution Facts

Municipal Pollution

- In 1995, most sewage (between 750 000 and 2 000 000 cubic metres daily) received only primary level treatment — filtering, settling, and removal of detergents — before being returned to the lower Fraser River and bays near its mouth.
- Less than one-tenth of the population is served by secondary level treatment plants, where sewage-eating bacteria consume waste products.
- There are 22 places along the lower Fraser where sewer systems can overflow untreated water into the river during heavy storm periods.

Industrial Pollution

- About one-half of the industrial discharge into the lower Fraser comes from the forest industry.
- Industries in the lower Fraser Valley hold Ministry of Environment permits to discharge a total of 300 000 cubic metres of waste water into the river daily.
- These industrial discharges can contain oils, grease, metals, and organic chemical compounds, some of them toxic.

Agricultural Pollution

- More than 600 000 cubic metres of farmland runoff enters the lower Fraser daily.
- Nutrients in animal and chemical fertilizers cause algae to grow in quiet stream areas.
- Decaying algae use up dissolved oxygen in the water, sometimes killing fish.

Source: Minister of Supply and Services, The State of Canada's Environment *(Ottawa: 1991), pp. XVI–15 to 18.*

FIGURE 3–22
Threatened species in the lower Fraser River valley.
Background: Snow Geese. These migratory birds winter in the delta marshes of the Fraser and the adjacent fields. Urban growth in these areas is destroying their habitat.

Pacific Salmon. In recent years fish numbers have declined, partly because of degrading water quality in the Fraser and other rivers.

Great Blue Heron. Scientists have measured steady increases in the level of toxic chemicals in the eggs of a colony of these large fishing birds near the University of British Columbia.

Lower Fraser Land-Use Issues

FIGURE 3–23

Intensive agriculture: a type of crop or tree farming that involves a lot of labour. Intensive agriculture is usually carried out on a small area, such as this cranberry bog, near Vancouver.

The lower Fraser Valley has the best quality farmland in British Columbia. It is used **intensively** for dairying, market gardening (vegetables), and specialty crops such as cranberries and mushrooms. Half the province's farm income is produced in this small area.

Urban growth in the valley has taken an average of 1500 hectares of farmland per year out of production since 1967. This is a total area equal to about 500 average-sized farms! The demand for real estate in the Vancouver area is so high that the value of the land itself is greater than a lifetime of crop earnings. Planners are aware of this problem and in recent years they have directed more urban expansion onto less productive land and unused urban lots. However, when this happens, it is wildlife habitat that is lost to metropolitan growth. As long as the Greater Vancouver area continues to grow, there will be difficult rural/urban land-use conflicts.

FIGURE 3–24

Extensive agriculture: a type of crop or livestock farming that does not use much labour in relation to the large area of the farm. Cattle ranching in B.C.'s interior is one example of extensive agriculture.

Legend

- ■ Water
- ■ Built-up areas
- ■ Mature forests
- ▨ Recently logged
- ▨ Cranberry bog
- ▨ Market gardening
- ▨ Dairying

N

CANADA
U.S.A.

FIGURE 3–25

Vancouver and the Fraser River delta. Find examples of farmland close to built-up areas. Why is this farmland worth a great deal of money? What other important values does this land have?

Can the Problems Be Solved?

Expanding residential and commercial areas create mountains of garbage. In 1995, it was estimated that all but one of the lower Fraser Valley landfill sites would be full by the year 2000. It is very difficult to open new landfills without public opposition; therefore, a rapid increase in recycling efforts is necessary. Industries in the Greater Vancouver area face even greater difficulties in safely disposing of toxic substances. Keeping these materials isolated from the water table and the Fraser River is especially important.

There is increasing need for parkland and fish and wildlife preserves in the lower Fraser Valley. Existing parkland in the area is heavily used. In 1995, the province, communities, wildlife agencies, and a forest company cooperated to create 1000 hectares of new parkland at 11 sites along the lower Fraser River. This was a small first step towards solving the environmental problems of the region.

Fraser Parkland Plan Praised

British Columbia's Environment Minister Moe Sihota was one of the politicians involved in the creation of the new parkland sites.

CREATING close to 1000 hectares of new parkland on the lower Fraser River at a cost of $28.5 million may not stop pollution or urban encroachment, but it is an important step in saving B.C.'s most important waterway.

That was the overwhelming response to an announcement Thursday by provincial, regional and municipal officials detailing park acquisitions at 11 sites on the lower Fraser between Abbotsford and Richmond.

The properties range from 10 hectares on Barnston Island, where bicyclists will finally receive such basic amenities as toilets and garbage cans, to 359-hectare Surrey Bend, an area of floodplain, forests, bog and meadows almost the size of Stanley Park.

"They're all great properties," said Mark Angelo, director of the Outdoor Recreation Council, which has listed the Fraser as the province's most endangered river.

• • •

Terry Slack, a gillnetter and environmental representative of the False Creek commercial fishing fleet, said he was especially pleased with the purchase of 187-hectare Douglas Island, 13-hectare Don and Lion Islands, as well as a 133-hectare addition to Iona Island Regional Park.

"All four provide important habitat for waterfowl and wetland birds, as well as an intertidal marsh area for juvenile salmon prior to their migration to the Pacific Ocean."

• • •

Some environmentalists agreed that, while the announcement dealt with property acquisition, it would also add pressure on government officials to curb pollution of the Fraser.

The most obvious example is the $650 million completion of the Greater Vancouver regional district's secondary sewage treatment plants at Annacis and Lulu islands. Thus far, less than half of the entire project has been financed and future construction is bogged down by intergovernmental bickering.

Source: L. Pynn, Vancouver Sun, May 5, 1995.

14. Use Figure 3–21 to answer the following questions:
    a) Find evidence to show that the ocean is shallow at the mouth of the Fraser River. Suggest some reasons why this area has become polluted.
    b) Find evidence that the land is mountainous north of the Fraser River. Prove that this area is important for recreation.
    c) Find evidence that the land south of the Fraser River is fairly flat. What important land uses would you expect to find in this area?
    d) Find evidence that most Vancouver-bound commuters come from east of the city. Explain why this is so.

15. Use the map scale (1:250 000 or 1 cm = 2.5 km) and major highways to estimate how far people travel to reach downtown Vancouver from each of the following:
    a) North Vancouver
    b) Richmond (Lulu Island)
    c) New Westminster
    d) Port Coquitlam
    e) Haney
    f) Langley

16. What effects is the rapid growth of Vancouver having upon each of the following?
    a) fish such as salmon
    b) waterfowl and small animals
    c) the Fraser River
    d) the Fraser River delta
    e) intensive farmland
    f) landfill sites

17. Use the display of Fraser River Pollution Facts to do one of the following activities.

    a) Draw an editorial cartoon critical of the situation.
    b) Write a letter to the local newspaper editor complaining about the problems.

18. Read the newspaper article "Fraser Parkland Plan Praised." Make a list of the problems that the new plan will help to solve. What are the shortcomings of the plan? Which serious environmental issues does the plan not address?

19. Work with a partner to examine the topographic map in Figure 3–21 and the satellite photo in Figure 3–25. They both show the same area.
    a) Locate the following features:
       • the Coast Range mountains
       • Fraser River
       • Burrard Inlet (the harbour)
       • Fraser River delta
       • Vancouver airport
       • forested areas
       • offshore sand deposits
       • residential areas
       • agricultural areas
       • central business district
    b) Make some decisions about future land uses. List your priorities for the use of the following:
       • forested areas in the Greater Vancouver area
       • delta lands of the Fraser River
       • rivers and bays around Greater Vancouver
       • sewage treatment and waste disposal in the region
    c) Use this information to write a letter to Greater Vancouver region officials, explaining the reasons for your land-use decisions.

PUTTING IT TOGETHER

Choose an urban community project:

1 Locate maps and photos of your own community (or one nearby) from different dates. Prepare a short illustrated report highlighting important changes the community has experienced during its history.

2 Use Census of Canada information from the local library to compare the characteristics of different neighbourhoods or communities in your area. Prepare number tables, graphs, and a short report of your findings.

3 Use newspapers and library files to gather information about environmental, social, political, and transportation issues in your community (or one nearby). Prepare an organized scrapbook with a short summary report.

4 Select one important issue in your community and apply the problem-solving wheel. Use the steps outlined in Figure 2–21 (page 31).